THE FILMMAKER'S JOURNEY

Or What Nobody Tells You About the Industry

By Chris Esper

Stories in Motion

www.storiesmotion.com

"Filled with fascinating topical life lessons, this ultimately inspiring work is an absolute must for those who dream of telling tales through the cinematic medium."

- Andrew Buckner, *A Word of Dreams*

"Not just a step-by-step guide to building a career in independent film, but one man's personal journey as seen through the camera lens. Chris Esper's enthusiasm as a film maker is infectious and his writing style follows suit. This book should prove to be as important to the next generation of film makers as Robert Rodriguez's Rebel Without A Crew *was to mine."*

- Chris Watt, Screenwriter and Film Critic, *Watch This Space Film Magazine*

"Esper shares his victories and struggles as an indie filmmaker with great candor, humility, and passion. I wish when I was starting out I would have heard these kinds of stories and known I wasn't alone in the many challenges that face new filmmakers! If you are new to filmmaking, read this right away!"

- Mikel J. Wisler, Author of *Short Films 2.0*

"This book gave me a greater understanding of the filmmaker's struggle. An ideal guide for any upcoming storyteller to keep moving forward."

- Dan Haddock, Film Critic, *The Local Film Network*

"There are more than a few 'how-to' guides out there about making indie films, so why should you check out another? The answer is that you need relevant and useful information, based on personal experience ('how I did it,' not 'how it should work in theory'). You want to hear from a credible, working filmmaker who tells it like it is, 'warts and all.' For practical advice based on hard lessons learned through actual indie filmmaking, Chris Esper's book is a must-read."

- Bill Meeker, Film Critic, *Loud Green Bird*

"In this book, Chris has told a warts-and-all tale of how he's succeeded and failed and succeeded again in carving out his niche in filmmaking. It's not only inspirational, but immensely helpful to those setting out on their own adventures in film."

- Brian Barnes, http://www.succeedingincorporates.co.uk

"An indispensable resource for the independent filmmaker."

- FilmFreeway

"I started No Entry Fee Festivals *to help good films get exposure and to encourage other filmmakers. In this same spirit, Chris Esper is sharing his resources and experiences to make the path a bit easier for his fellow artists."*

-Tracy Miller-Robbins, noentryfeefestivals.com

The Filmmaker's Journey: Or What Nobody Tells You

About the Industry

Copyright © Stories in Motion 2016. All Rights

Reserved.

Published by the author

www.storiesmotion.com

First edition: April 2016

Copy Editor: Eric Bumpus

Line Editor: William Meeker

Cover Design: Chris Esper

All Rights Reserved. No part of this publication may be reproduced, stored in a retrieval system, or transmitted in any form or by any means—such as electronic, photocopy, recording—without the prior written consent of the author. The only exception is brief quotations in reviews, both printed and electronic.

For Mom and Dad

TABLE OF CONTENTS

ACKNOWLEDGEMENTS

CHAPTER 1: MY STORY

CHAPTER 2: PICK UP THE CAMERA AND GO!

CHAPTER 3: IT'S NOT OVER YET

CHAPTER 4: REJECTION, REJECTION, REJECTION

CHAPTER 5: LOCATION, LOCATION, LOCATION

CHAPTER 6: GET PAID FOR YOUR PASSION

CHAPTER 7: THE IMPORTANCE OF FEEDBACK

CHAPTER 8: SURROUND YOURSELF WITH THE RIGHT PEOPLE

CHAPTER 9: WHAT IT MEANS TO BE A DIRECTOR

CHAPTER 10: TECHNOLOGY AND FILMMAKING

CHAPTER 11: DO IT FOR THE RIGHT REASONS

CHAPTER 12: FINAL THOUGHTS

APPENDIX: RESOURCES AND REFERENCES

ACKNOWLEDGEMENTS

I have spent years reading about filmmaking. I never thought I would see the day where I would be writing my own book about a subject that is so close to my heart and yet so difficult to understand as a career. So I have to acknowledge those who have supported my work and my endeavors over the years.

First, I have to thank my best friend, Rich Camp. I met Rich in 2010 when he was looking for interns to work on a feature comedy he was making. I was 20 years old at the time and had never worked on a film set. What started out as an internship blossomed into a friendship. Rich has been there through all my ups and downs. He was the first person to be tough with me and has been a big part of my growth as a filmmaker. He has also given me numerous opportunities to show what I can do by having me direct material he had written.

I also have to thank my dear friend and producing partner, Creusa Michelazzo, who owns and operates Macremi Productions. Creusa has been and continues to be my rock. She's always there to lift me up when I'm down and to inspire me to continue when I feel like quitting. She's also the first person to bring me back to reality whenever I get too full of myself.

I must also thank those who have been generous with their feedback as I wrote this book: Felipe Jorge, Aaron Olsen, Mikel J. Wisler, and Brian R. Boisvert. Also, special thanks to Eric Bumpus, William Meeker, and Leah Gage for their hard work in editing the book and to the film critics and filmmakers who have been kind enough to endorse this piece.

Finally, I have to acknowledge my family, especially my parents, George and Rita Esper. They not only gave me life, but also instilled their work ethic into me. I'll never forget the moments when I would excitedly show them my high school films and how much they have encouraged me to follow such a crazy career choice.

Chapter 1: My Story

I have been making films for only six years, but during these six years I have learned a lot and continue to do so. This is my rationale for writing this book. I want to share my story and all that I have learned.

I call this *The Filmmaker's Journey* because that is exactly what this career is: a journey. There are peaks and valleys throughout; things never go according to plan. I am basing this book on my 'vlog'[1] of the same name where I give similar advice. However, there are often a lot of things I can't cover in my videos because I can't explain them in five minutes or less. So this book is a better way of expressing these larger ideas. It also includes my insights beyond those I put out on the Internet.

Before you continue, know that this is not going to be a how-to book on how to make a movie. There is

---

[1] *The Filmmaker's Journey* 'vlog'

plenty of information out there on that topic. To be honest, I can't teach you how to make a movie because there isn't an exact formula. Every filmmaker has a different way of working. The only way to learn is by doing. I am also not going to be recommending pieces of gear or equipment. Filmmaking should be about telling the story and advancing in your career. And with that...

I was born and raised in New Jersey. I lived in a small town where everybody knew everybody. I had a fun childhood. Part of that enjoyment came from movies. I lived across the street from a video store, Broadway Video, just off of 31st Street in Bayonne. Between going to the video store and my parents taking me to the theater, I was captivated by movies from a young age. I used to walk across the street on my own to rent several movies at a time. I always discovered something new.

The first girl I ever had a crush on worked at Broadway Video. Her name was Veronica. She had beautiful brown hair and brown eyes. I used to try so hard to make conversation with her by talking about what I knew best: movies. I was ten or twelve years old; she could have very well been in her late teens or early twenties. She probably had no idea why I was talking to her. Why was I trying to win her over by talking about movies when she was surrounded by them all day? I believe that this first crush played into the romantic approach that I take not only to women but also to film itself.

Around that time, I was considering getting into acting and comedy much like the late Robin Williams, whom I considered my favorite actor at that age. Also, I had seen *Ghostbusters* and really enjoyed it, as well as other science fiction comedies; so I decided to write a screenplay in that genre.

I went about writing a thirty-page script entitled *Boy Bot*. The story was about a young boy genius who invents a robot and has to fight aliens. Since I did not know anything about the movie business, I believed that this could be a feature film. I told all my fourth-grade friends that I was making a movie and that they were going to be part of it. They were really excited--everybody wanted to be in it.

The next thing I did was probably the gutsiest thing a ten year old could do. I went on IMDb, found the name of the producer of *Ghostbusters* at Columbia Pictures, and sent him my screenplay. I had no clue that a studio would never accept an unsolicited script. But I was hell-bent on making it happen.

Days turned to weeks, weeks turned to months, and still no response. One day, I came home from school to discover the yellow envelope I had sent in the mailbox with "Return to Sender" stamped on it. To this day, I still have that screenplay. Every once in a while I take a look at it. It's terrible writing, but it provided an opportunity for self-discovery. Many have said that I should revive it and turn it into a movie. Maybe one day--who knows?

When I was fourteen, I moved to Rhode Island where my life's passion slowly started to take shape. Throughout high school, I tried out different forms of art, from acting in the drama club to doing stand-up comedy and puppetry. Eventually, I got my first camera, which was nothing more than a mini-DVD camera. I was seventeen years old.

At the time, YouTube was becoming a big deal. Being able to upload videos online to a large public audience was something new. No one had ever seen anything like this. With my first camera, I made a variety of creations, including a stop motion animated logo of my "production company," Chris Esper Productions. The logo consisted of a clay figure of myself walking to the camera to discover the letter "C" was missing in my name. "Where's the C?!" my voice exclaimed. The missing letter then came down on a hook and hit the figure in the head. It was a fun and cute creation that became my calling card with my classmates.

Then I moved on to live action pictures by making a documentary about stand-up comedy at the club where I had once performed. Soon I was making narrative films.

I created short experimental and sometimes dialogue-driven films. I did everything by myself, from writing to directing, shooting, editing, effects, and acting. It was a silly looking operation, but it worked. Without realizing it, I was learning different techniques.

One of my most memorable situations occurred when I was making a Chaplin-esque silent comedy. The film was about a man who couldn't open his door because he forgot his keys, and he tries different ways to get the door open. There I was, dressed in a 1920's-like outfit on my porch with my camera set up on one side. I hit record, did the action and then cut camera. I set up another angle and did it again (and again) until it was over.

Neighbors passed by, looking at me like I was some alien being. Meanwhile, my family was inside hearing me make noises and banging on the door. No one had a clue what I was doing or why.

My school friends did not always understand why I was making movies, but some were impressed. Eventually I showed everyone the silent film. That was when everyone saw what they thought was a hobby turning into something serious. It was also the moment when my parents told me I had talent. It was amazing to get that validation.

All the while, I was also becoming a movie buff. I eventually went from enjoying movies for teens and young adults, to appreciating the classics and more artistic cinema. When I saw *Raging Bull*, I knew for sure that filmmaking was the career I was going to pursue. I listened to Martin Scorsese's commentary and watched the "making-of" documentary. It inspired me to hear Scorsese talk about the ideas he had while making the movie, versus what he had intended to do.

It was then that I realized that movies were more than just entertainment; film was an art form. At eighteen years old, I knew what I wanted to do with my life: I wanted to make movies. I realized right away that by making films, I could incorporate everything I loved: acting, comedy, puppetry, animation, writing, photography, and the arts in general. I could combine it all into one medium.

In 2009, I started college at the New England Institute of Technology, where I studied film and video. I graduated in 2012 with a Bachelor's Degree in Digital Recording Arts. During my time in school, I started getting my name out into the New England filmmaking scene. While I was working on student projects and showing them at festivals, I was also working on other filmmakers' sets as assistant cameraman, camera operator, sound mixer, editor, production assistant, grip, etc. I probably did everything except hair and make-up.

When I graduated, I started making films with a crew, aiming to get my work out to a bigger audience. I began by making a twelve-minute drama called *Still Life*[2], in which a photography student struggles with his negative thoughts about his creativity and talent. It was a personal story based on my experience of questioning myself and my abilities as a filmmaker. The film ended up receiving a standing ovation at a local screening, which was a very rewarding experience. It also received praise from film critics and ended up playing in eight film festivals around the country.

I continued to make films and win awards at festivals. I also started doing videography work for a living. I'll tell you more about my experiences and what I learned during my internship in later chapters.

Currently, I am hard at work writing my first feature screenplay, getting my short comedy film

---

[2] *Still Life*, directed by Chris Esper, 2012, available at www.storiesmotion.com

(*Please Punish Me*)[3] on the festival circuit, wrapping my latest short film (*A Very Proper Man*) and building up my production company, Stories in Motion.

---

[3] *Please Punish Me*, directed by Chris Esper, 2015, trailer available at www.storiesmotion.com

CHAPTER 2: PICK UP THE CAMERA AND GO!

I cannot stress this chapter's title enough. As I sit here typing, I'm thinking I should be writing a screenplay or filming a small project. But over the years I have made many excuses about why I cannot make a movie. I hear others doing the same. Do these sound familiar?

"I don't have the money."

"I don't have the equipment."

"I didn't go to film school."

"I don't live in LA."

"I don't have a good script."

"I don't know how to fix that script."

Etc., etc., etc.

These excuses go on and on, but they're just a waste of time and energy. There is no excuse good enough to keep you from making a movie. Just look on YouTube or Vimeo and you'll see how many people are making movies these days. That is because there is more filmmaking technology readily and easily available than ever before.

Twenty or thirty years ago, making a movie on little to no budget was almost impossible. Video cameras were not always able to produce the cinematic quality for which one would hope. These days you can even make a quality, little to no budget film on your iPhone.

In 2014, at the Sundance Film Festival in Utah, a film called *Tangerine* [4] screened. It was a big hit at the festival, and afterwards was able to acquire a distribution deal. Perhaps the most surprising thing about the film was that **it was shot entirely on an iPhone**, yet it was able to achieve a cinematic look and feel. It looked good because its makers took the time to light it and color grade it correctly, along with capturing quality sound. You can do this too. The tools don't make

---

[4] *Tangerine*, directed by Sean Baker, 2014, trailer available on YouTube.

the movie, the moviemaker does. You don't need to go to film school either. All you need to do is to keep making movies.

That is not to say that film school doesn't have its benefits. For one thing, if you go to film school you'll be able to work with like-minded people who love movies and filmmaking. Everyone is willing to help one another. You also make a lot of connections that could lead you to jobs in New York City, L.A. or elsewhere. You also get invaluable on-set experience.

The decision about whether or not film school is right for you is yours to make. I cannot tell you what will work for you. Some do better learning in a hands-on environment; others do better in the classroom and with books. I have always been a hands-on person and so I went to a technical college. New England Tech is not a film school, but it had courses about film. I also did a lot of research on my own time and taught myself by working on sets and making short films.

I really wanted to go to a "real" film school like New York University (NYU) or its peers, but 1) I couldn't afford it and 2) it didn't feel right for me. Every once in a while, I struggle with regrets that I did not attend a better college to really focus on film, assuming that I would have made more connections or even better films. I always decide these misgivings are false.

Much like the equipment, the school doesn't make the filmmaker either. Your artistry is within you and can be refined over time as you grow in your craft. When I was in L.A., I went to a screening of student films at the Director's Guild. They were quite good on most levels. I have to admit that I was jealous of them.

When I tried to approach one of the student filmmakers to congratulate him, I found that he had this really annoying, pretentious vibe to him. He kept trying to tell me how the film school he attended was the way to go and that I should apply if I wanted to be a successful filmmaker. I was polite and thanked him for the recommendation, but he kept shoving the idea down my throat. Following his advice was the last thing I wanted to do.

Film school also does not guarantee a job when you graduate, no matter where you go. There are tons of people who go to film school and then attempt to work their way up the system. They start as a production assistant on a lot of sets, hoping to eventually become a director. As good as that sounds, if you want to make movies, what are you doing being a production assistant? If you want to make movies, then make your own. Don't wait.

No one is going to give you permission to make movies except yourself. Don't wait for the money, equipment, or a degree. Don't wait for anything. Put down this book and start working on that movie. Then come back when you're done.

Chapter 3: It's Not Over Yet

When you finish your movie, you're probably wondering how you get it out there. Let's start with film festivals.

Film festivals are a great way to get your film in front of as many eyeballs as possible. Being accepted into a festival of any kind makes your film look good. You'll meet a lot of other film people at festivals, and best of all, your movie gets seen by an audience. Sounds easy enough, right? Hell, no.

I love film festivals and showing my work at them, but getting accepted into one is like trying to get into an Ivy League college. I have received more rejections than acceptances, quite honestly. I submitted one film to forty festivals and got into six. On a different occasion, I submitted to twenty-four and got into three. It's a numbers game. Many good films don't make the cut because of any number of reasons, but don't let that stop you. Here are some tips on how you can better your chances of getting into festivals.

First, the worst thing you can do is blindly submit to multiple festivals without knowing which ones your film is a good fit for. Every festival has a niche audience to which accepted films cater. Festival organizers need to sell tickets, after all. The best thing you can do to increase your chances of being accepted is a lot of research.

Look at past films that a festival has accepted (even if all you can find is a trailer) to get an idea of what the organizers are looking for. You can even send a clip or trailer of your own film to festival organizers and ask them if it's the kind of thing they're looking for. There's no reason for paying an entry fee to a festival if your film does not have a chance of acceptance.

I found that out the hard way. I submitted one of my dramas to a festival that accepts only fantasy films. Had I read the rules first, I would not have been rejected. So come up with a plan of attack for where to submit beforehand.

If you do get accepted, congrats! That's a big accomplishment, even if the festival is small. Any festival builds your career by giving you opportunities to make connections. When you go, be sure to bring business cards, have fun and most of all, network with people. Also make sure to follow up with the people you meet.

If you do get rejected, do not -- **I repeat, do not** -- contact the festival with an angry e-mail. It is the absolute worst thing anyone can do, and burn bridges. The next time you submit to them, they will remember who you are and how you behaved. Remember to be professional and either ignore the rejections, or contact the festival's organizers to ask for feedback. Then, you'll be able to use that feedback the next time you make a film.

Another thing to remember: just because a festival rejected your film does not necessarily mean that the organizers did not like your film. The reason could have been that your film was too long, not quite what they were looking for, or some additional reason other than quality. There were a few times when I contacted festivals to ask for feedback and received positive comments. Their reasons for rejection were due to time constraints and little things like that. It simply turned out that my film wasn't right for those festivals that particular year.

Where can you submit? There are tons of websites. Film Freeway is the one I use the most. It is user-friendly and convenient for all parties involved in the process. Before using Film Freeway, I used Withoutabox, as most filmmakers have. Over the years, the site has gotten better and more user-friendly. Another great one is No Entry Fee Festivals, which lists festivals that are all free to enter and submit. If you cannot afford to submit to a lot of festivals, this is a great option.

Besides live festival events, there are also online film festivals, such as Short of the Week, out of New York. It screens content from all over the world. Whether your film is accepted or rejected, they give you feedback on your project. I also recommend The Online Film Festival. Again, they have content from all over and the great thing about this site is that your community can support you by voting for your film.

Another great way to get your film out into the world is through online film critics. Film critics not only review your film, but also provide publicity for your film through the articles they write. People who read their articles often begin to follow your work, especially if you got a positive review. Even if your film gets trashed, it's still press.

If you do get a bad review, do not respond in anger. Thank the critic for his or her time, especially if you reached out to them in the first place. With big-name Hollywood filmmakers, the critics seek out the films, but the same is not true with independent filmmakers. We have to make the first move.

Take whatever feedback a critic gives you and use it to your advantage. For me, film critics are not just good for promotional reasons. It's also great to have somebody you don't know, who is not a peer, give you an honest review. It feels good when your filmmaker peers rave about your film, but how honest are they being with you? Keep that in mind -- we will discuss feedback in another chapter.

The point is: if you get a bad review, thank the critic for taking the time to watch and review your film. Then turn that negative into a positive. I had a film reviewed by a film critic in the UK who did not like the film at all. He had nothing positive to say. This truly hurt in a big way.

My initial reaction was anger and sadness. However, rather than directing these feelings towards the critic, I found him on Twitter, followed him and sent him a tweet. I thanked him for reviewing the film and told him that I looked forward to showing him what else I have to offer in the future. To my surprise, he not only thanked me back, but he shared my tweet on his Facebook page with the following caption:

"That moment when the director of the film you gave a bad review to not only follows you on Twitter, but turns out to be a nice and smart guy. #Bridgebuilding."

This reviewer has continued to follow me and my work. He has liked the subsequent films I have sent his way and even interviewed me on his website. He describes me as, "a talented filmmaker who is a class act."

One small act of kindness can go a long way in your career when you remain professional in the midst of a bad situation. With all that said, in the appendix of this book you will find a master list of all the film critics

I have submitted to and continue to contact. You can send your films to them as well.

One last option to get your film out there is distribution. With the advent of digital technology, it is becoming increasingly easier to get your film seen by the world. From YouTube to Vimeo, to the big boys like Netflix, Amazon Prime or Hulu, you have lots of options. The great thing about these websites is that you can get instant results and reach a large crowd within a short period of time. Getting the audience is the hard part, but if you keep posting content, you will gain a following.

A couple years ago, I discovered a website called Distribber,[5] where you can submit your project to be considered for Netflix, Hulu, iTunes, Redbox and more. It is not cheap, but it's worth it. This is especially true for those out there making feature films. Short films have some distribution avenues, but not enough to make money. Short films are not profitable. They are

---

[5] Distribber Official Website: www.distribber.com

best at helping you to perfect your craft and for showcasing what you and your actors can do. They can certainly lead to feature film projects. No matter how you distribute your film, make sure the platform you choose is right for your project.

When I finished *Still Life*[6] in 2012 and it started playing on the festival circuit, I was pretty proud of what it accomplished. One night when I was on Facebook, one of my filmmaking friends posted about a new and upcoming online distribution company looking for content, including short films. I got curious, so I submitted, not thinking anything of it. I then received a message later that night informing me that the company enjoyed my film and wanted to feature it as part of their short film library. I was both shocked and flattered.

Did my $500 short film just get a distribution offer? I had to process this for a while. Then I looked closer at the website. It was clearly primitive and still

---

[6] *Still Life*, directed by Chris Esper, 2012, available at www.storiesmotion.com

under construction. I didn't want to judge it prematurely, but I was skeptical. Then I noticed a few films on the site by a local director whom I had met a few months prior. I contacted this filmmaker and asked him what he thought of the service and whether he felt it was on the up and up. He did.

So, with that in mind, I started to seriously consider the possibility of getting distribution for my short. Of course, like any young filmmaker, I was excited and wanted to sign the contract right away. I wanted to brag about it. I called the distributor the next day and that is when things started to become clear. The man I talked to seemed excited about my film and the company he was starting. I started to believe in him until he told me about the compensation.

He had asked that the directors of the short films to pay $200 to get their film distributed. They would receive 10% of the profits generated by the website, even if nobody rented or bought their film. Feature filmmakers would need to pay $400 to get their film distributed and would receive 60% of the site's profits.

Alarm bells went off in my head. At the same time, I kept trying to reason away my negative thoughts. It seemed like too good of an opportunity to pass up. I talked about it with everyone I knew. They were all thrilled for me, but told me not to do it because of the money involved. I didn't listen. I paid the $200, told everyone on social media and felt great about it.

Months later, my first check from the company came in the mail. Guess how much I made? **A whopping $5.50.** That's right. I made $5.50 off my $200 investment. And it doesn't end there.

I still had hope that the site would generate more subscribers. During the summer, the distributor came up to Boston to host a dinner party. He tried to get more people on board to invest in the company and gain more followers. I attended this party along with all my film friends and collaborators. Everything was going well until the distributor started talking and told everyone that they were looking for any films they could get and now submission was free for filmmakers. I quickly blurted out a "What?!" at that statement and he apologized to me as if it was no big deal.

I took him aside afterwards and asked him who watched my film and why it was picked. I was genuinely curious if my film truly deserved to be there or if I was just a placeholder to show that there is content. I also wanted my money back. He told me that he watched the film himself and that he enjoyed it. He then assured me that the money would be coming in and to be patient. I didn't want to ruin his party, so I just listened and nodded my head.

A few months later, nothing had changed with this website. No money was being made for anybody, even after we did a lot of promoting. Filmmakers were even given discount code cards to hand out. Nothing was working. I stopped promoting the movie and just continued submitting to festivals -- which, by the way the distributor kept telling me I did not need to do because of his site. One festival turned me down because I had distribution for my film, even though they liked it. Eventually, I stopped caring.

Later, I got an e-mail from a film critic who I had asked to review my film. He said the distribution site I had posted the film on was down and asked if I had another link to provide. I quickly went online: the website was indeed gone. I checked the Facebook page for updates. Gone. The entire existence of this "company" had been erased for good.

I tried to call the distributor, but he didn't pick up. I left a voice mail message and then I sent him a text message and an email. Again, I did not hear a thing back from him. I contacted one of my good friends who had three films on the site, a $600 investment for him. He also had heard nothing. Our hopes and dreams of being one of the few to make money off of our short films were gone. We never heard from him again.

Many are probably reading this and wondering why none of us sued. Well, all the evidence was gone and while we had our contracts, he never actually violated them. We did receive our first quarterly payment, as contracted. What could we do? It was over.

The moral of this story is that you should not rush to get your film out there, especially if an offer sounds too good to be true. Think about it and think about it some more before signing anything or paying anything. But don't let my story get you down. There are tremendous opportunities out there to get your film seen. Each one is great in its own way. Just know that your film is different from all the rest and you need to market it right. It is through experiences like this that I feel I became a better businessman as well as filmmaker. Again, it's about taking those negative experiences and turning them into positive ones.

Chapter 4: Rejection, Rejection, Rejection

Get used to rejection because you are going to get a lot of it. You're going to get a million "no"s before you get one "yes". How do you deal with that rejection and find the strength to continue? Believe me, it is far from easy.

There was one week a couple years ago when I heard from five film festivals over three days. Each one rejected my film. It was heartbreaking. I was ready to quit right then and there. Then I got an acceptance one month later and gained my confidence back. I got rejected once more after that and was heartbroken again.

This is a career with no straight road and many detours. So before you decide to put your film out there or even consider making one, just keep that in mind. I wish somebody had told me that before I started. I don't think I would have been as heartbroken or sad.

To me, the best way to handle rejection is to simply keep going without even thinking about it. The moment you start thinking about a rejection, you put yourself in a position where you feel like you want to give up. If you do come to a point where you feel you can't take it anymore and you don't know what to do, go back to the thing that made you want to make movies. Trust me, that will reinvigorate you.

When you get rejected, you will likely end up comparing yourself negatively to other filmmakers who may be successful. I did it all the time and still find myself doing that. It is probably the worst thing you can do to yourself. First of all, you are your own person as a filmmaker; your path will not be the same as another's. Also, if you take a moment to do a Google search on rejection letters for famous people, you will find pages of results. The problem is that whenever we read or learn about our film idols, we never look for their failures like we should. It will put things in perspective that even they went through the same struggles.

One day, while I was in L.A., I was feeling really down about the direction my career was going. As I was on my computer, I came across a video somebody posted of Martin Scorsese giving a commencement speech to the NYU graduates[7]. Since Scorsese is my filmmaking idol, I watched it right away. It was an extremely eye-opening forty minutes. It reminded me that I am not the only one who has gone through hardships.

Scorsese talked about a situation he had when he was trying to get an investor to fund his first feature film. He and his producer at the time showed the investor a series of short films that they had made during their time at NYU. The investor walked out of the screening room with a smile on his face and laughing. Thinking that this was good news, Scorsese and his producer approached him and asked him what he thought. The investor said, "I didn't like it." "Which one didn't you like? *The Big Shave*? It won a lot of student

---

[7] Martin Scorsese NYU Commencement Speech, 2014: www.vimeo.com/106196480

awards and was a big hit at the New York Film Festival," the producer pressed on. "One joke film," the investor replied. "How about *It's Not Just You, Murray?* It won a lot of awards and played at New York film festivals," said the producer. "I didn't like that either," said the investor. He then leaned in closer to Scorsese and said, "If I saw one thread of talent in there, I would tell you. But I did not." With that, he left with a smile still on his face. I had not heard this story before and was amazed. At the same time, I was shaking my head, feeling the pain that I am sure Scorsese felt.

Here is another story for you. Another day in L.A., I had this huge sense of determination. I printed thirty copies of my resume and hit the streets to go door-to-door to a series of companies I had mapped out. I spent the whole day doing this. At each place, they said the same things:

"We're not hiring."
"You're not from here."

"We can't take applications. You have to go online to apply."

I kept hearing the same things over and over again. Now to be fair, some of the places I visited did indeed take my resume, but I was surprised that many did not. I even lied and told them that I did apply online, but nobody contacted me, so I decided to come in person. It didn't matter. At one point I even ended up at Fox Studios and went inside. Nobody said a word.

Sometimes you need to go all out and do as much as you can to find acceptance within the industry no matter where you are. Either way, rejection is part of the business. But it gets easier. As I write this, I have received three rejections in the last couple of days. I have come to realize that it does not mean you are not talented; it just means that it is not your time yet or there is a better opportunity out there for you.

CHAPTER 5: LOCATION, LOCATION, LOCATION

The big question everybody asks about getting into the film business is whether or not you need to move to L.A. or N.Y.C. That is not a very easy question to answer, but I will say this: You can make a movie anywhere and still receive attention for it.

I come from New England, which many refer to as Hollywood East. I don't know how true that is, but my peers and I have gotten many opportunities and found some success by being in New England. Not only that, but New England has been a home to some Hollywood productions. *Underdog*, *Ghostbusters (2016)*, both *Ted* movies and so many others gave New England crew members and actors work. It's a great hub of people who are all passionate about filmmaking, but it's not L.A.

What many don't realize is that New England is where movies can be filmed, but it is not where the Mecca of filmmaking is located. L.A. is where the business is done. It is where you meet the people you need to know in order to turn your passion into a career.

The reason movies get filmed in New England or other locations is because there are tax incentives to entice productions to shoot there. In the six years I have been working in the New England film community, I have found some paid work, but I would be lying if I said I was making millions and got a deal with Paramount. I did, however, go to L.A. for a three-month internship with OddLot Entertainment (*Drive, Way, Way Back, Draft Day*).

I got the internship through the Moving Picture Institute's (MPI) Hollywood Career Launch Program. MPI is a non-profit organization that promotes freedom and liberty through film. Their program looks for interns who want to work for a company in either L.A. or N.Y.C. for a three-month period and with pay. I was lucky enough to be accepted into the program and then selected by OddLot Entertainment to be their intern. It was a fantastic learning experience on both professional and personal levels.

My main job at OddLot was writing script coverage. For those that don't know, script coverage consists of reading a screenplay that has been submitted to determine if it's one to pass on, consider, or recommend. It was a great way to learn about storytelling and also what kind of stuff a studio looks for in a script.

Every week we had trailer meetings where we would watch trailers and discuss them. We would also analyze the box office numbers from the previous weekend. Those were fun events. But my other tasks included taking lunch orders, answering phones and making coffee in the morning. For many, these would seem like thankless jobs. While doing these small tasks, I realized that they put me in frequent contact with key people. Being known by these people is the first step to getting future recommendations.

I realize I said earlier that you should not have to do the small jobs, such as being a P.A., to be able to make movies, but I didn't mean you should not do them at all. I wanted to make sure I stood out as much as possible, including reporting to work at 8:00 A.M. when I was supposed to be there at 9:00 A.M. This seemed to impress the office manager and others. So if you are looking to get your start in L.A., I highly recommend doing an internship or something small while you also make your projects. You will get noticed no matter what. Go to MPI's website[8] to apply to their internship program.

Even though I was in LA to be an intern, I made sure that I took full advantage of opportunities that came my way while I was there. I went to a couple of networking events and film screenings at the Director's Guild. I even managed to get two of my films accepted into a festival. One film walked away with the Best Comedy Short award.

---

[8] Moving Picture Institute: www.thempi.org

Yet nothing was more gratifying than meeting one of my favorite directors, Kenneth Johnson (*The Incredible Hulk (1978-1982), V (1983), Short Circuit 2)*. I had been following Johnson's work for a number of years and had emailed him a few times with questions. I even sent him a copy of one of my films. This time around, I had e-mailed him to let him know I was in L.A. and that I would love to meet him in person and perhaps pick his brain a little. To my surprise, he said yes and proceeded to invite me to his office.

The following week I found myself in his office, surrounded by posters of his work and memorabilia, feeling like a kid in a candy store. We talked for about an hour. He told me many stories about his start in the business, as well as some behind-the-scenes anecdotes. One of the things he noted was that it's all about who you know; you have to do anything you can to network your way in.

When I asked him how one starts a career as a director and actually gets paid for it, his advice was to just keep making movies and don't wait. He also mentioned getting training at the Director's Guild by becoming an assistant director trainee and working my way up from there. After our meeting, he invited me to attend his directing class as his guest at the New York Film Academy in Burbank. I had heard about this class for years and always wanted to go, so I was thrilled to be invited.

It was a fantastic class. He showed clips of his work and described how a scene was done. He was also very hands-on with the students, showing how a movie is made and what goes into it. Oh, and in case you were wondering: Yes, he did watch my film and he liked it! I highly suggest going to his website[9] to find out when his next class is scheduled.

The reason I tell you this: If you have idols in the business, reach out to them. You may be surprised how willing a lot of them are to meet you. I contacted other

---

[9] Kenneth Johnson's website: www.kennethjohnson.us

writers and filmmakers like Kenneth Johnson not long after that. Most of them answered me and agreed to talk either through email or in person. It is refreshing to hear your idols give you encouragement and/or teach you in some way.

MPI was also quite instrumental in giving me opportunities to learn and meet people outside my internship. Screenwriter John Truby,[10] who wrote the TV series *21 Jump Street*, was giving a seminar on screenwriting and volunteers were needed to help with the event. Volunteers were also invited to be able to sit in on the class for free. I was lucky enough to get the job. I spent three days volunteering and watching Truby breakdown screenplays beat by beat. It was a terrific learning experience that left an impression on me.

Soon afterward, I had the chance to work at one of the major studios (I cannot say which) for a week doing post-production work on an independent movie being made there. The only reason I got the job was

---

[10] John Truby's website: www.truby.com

because I knew someone who worked at the studio and he needed somebody with post-production experience to help him. I jumped on board right away. Like Johnson said, it is all about who you know. The thing about L.A.-- or anywhere, for that matter-- is that you can have the greatest resume and all the talent in the world, but it doesn't matter. I wouldn't have gotten the jobs or opportunities I did if I did not network or put myself out there.

No matter where you're located, make it a point to meet as many people as possible and network your way in. Nobody is going to look out for you, so it is all up to you. In the end, I definitely say to give L.A. a chance if you have the opportunity, even if it's just for a week or so. Apply for jobs and network as much as possible. N.Y.C. and Atlanta, GA are also great options.

If you can't afford to go to one of these cities, you can make movies in your current location. You would be surprised what you can do. Every state has at least one filmmaking group you can go to for help, whether it be for crew members or actors. See the appendix for filmmaking groups.

Chapter 6: Get Paid for Your Passion

How nice would it be to get paid to make your passion projects? I think every filmmaker has this dream. When you make movies on the independent level, it is hard to raise money and even harder to make money back on that investment. So, how do you make money from your movies?

If you want to be a director, that's great, but also make it a priority to learn all aspects of production, from pre-production through post-production. Also, learn the technical aspects of shooting, lighting, sound recording, and editing. You do not have to do all these things at once, but there are situations where you may need to, such as the case with videography.

If you want to make money making films, your answer might be in videography. I know, I know, that does not sound nearly as glamorous as filmmaking, but you would be surprised at what kind of money you can make doing videography. You can find a variety of jobs in videography such as: editing demo reels for actors, shooting weddings and events, and doing commercial projects such as advertisements, corporate training, and music videos. Each one provides opportunities to try different things that you might not always get to do in a movie production. Everything you learn can later be applied to your next passion project.

I should also add that just because you are doing an industrial or promotional video does not mean that you are stripped of your creativity. You can use your creativity to make a somewhat cinematic video. Obviously, you will need to listen to what the client wants and will need to work within their budget, but you can put your own spin on the video. The idea of doing videography is not often a fun one, but if you can make it enjoyable for yourself while exceeding your client's expectations, then everybody wins. If you are not enjoying yourself, it will be reflected in your work.

Over the past three years, I have made a lot of connections and gained more work and experience by freelancing as a videographer. It has given me the opportunity, knowledge and money to make the films I hoped to make. I have worked for six wedding companies, shot and edited demo reels for actors, made commercials, music videos and more. All have proven to be great ways to make a living. The only downside can be working with the client.

I have been blessed with the clients for whom I have worked. Most have been terrific and easy to work with. They also trusted my creativity and vision. I did have one client, though, who was far from a great experience. It was not my first client, either. In 2015, a man was looking to make a music video for his daughter's new song. It would be their first video. He was asking around for recommendations for videographers and my name came up a number of times. This man finally contacted me and explained what he was looking for.

He asked me to listen to the song to see if I liked it. I did listen to it; I thought it was okay. Not horrible, but I didn't see it being on the Billboard Top 100. Wanting to expand myself more, I decided to meet with him and his daughter. The meeting went well overall. They had seen one of my previous music videos and liked it. They were especially impressed by the fact that it won an award at a film festival. This is when I started to worry a little.

The moment the accolades start coming into play, you know the project is not being done for the right reasons. They had a budget of $1,000 to spend, but had a vision for a $10,000 video. One of their ideas was to do a complicated 360-degree shot with special effects. I was also asked if I could use my LA connections to get the video out there. All these things left me concerned. Despite these feelings, I decided to give them a chance.

I gathered together a crew and helped them scout locations. During this process I got phone call after phone call, in which the client pestered me about every detail. I had never experienced anything quite like this. I was getting annoyed, but I just assured the client that we were going to be fine.

He was especially concerned about the 360-degree shot he wanted to get. I told him from the beginning that I would look into it, but that it sounded very complex for the budget we had to work with. My crew agreed with me and thought that we should scrap it altogether in favor of another idea. I ran this by the client, but he wasn't interested in compromise. I always try to please the client, but in this case I knew we were going to have problems. I didn't want to give in that easily. I suggested trying different special effects to get the same idea across without doing the complex shot. I showed the father and daughter some examples of what I was talking about. They deflected or shot down each of them. To them, it either looked cheap or too simple. They wanted-- and I quote -- "something that looks better than what you see on social media or MTV." Sorry, but for $1,000 that cannot be done.

Clearly, this was a client with unrealistic expectations. I tried to communicate my concerns once again. After pushing and pushing, they finally agreed to go with an alternative plan. I thought the worst was over, but that was hardly the case.

The first day of shooting came. Prior to that, I had scouted locations with the client and took photos. We were all set to go, or so I thought. While I was on my way to the first location, I got a call from my cinematographer, who arrived a few minutes before I did. She told me the location was private, according to a tiny sign she saw that I somehow missed. The client had informed me that it was public property and no permits would be needed. I took his word for it, because he lives in the town we were shooting. I got there and, sure enough, there was the tiny sign. My cinematographer refused to shoot due to the fear of being shut down. I was in complete agreement with her.

The clients arrived about ten minutes later. We informed them about what was going on. The father did not understand how this would be a problem because he lives in the town. We explained that if we had known it was private, we would have obtained a permit or at least informed the property owners, none of whom we knew. So, our only option was to regroup and go to the next scheduled location. In the meantime, we had to find a new location to replace the one that was private property.

The rest of the day went fine, for the most part, but we had one more day of shooting left. Originally, we had planned to shoot the next day. However, we needed to find a location for the next day's shoot. It was the hardest one to find. We ended up rescheduling for the following week.

As we approached the rescheduled shooting day, it was becoming more and more apparent that we were not going to be able to get the type of location that we wanted. The client's vision was very specific. All we needed was a living room, but it is hard enough to find homeowners willing to let you film, let alone find a big living room with large windows. These specific ideas can easily back you into a tight corner.

On top of this, the client was again asking that we do the 360-degree shot. At one point, he even suggested shooting the scene in a gazebo in a public outdoor mall because it was round. This would not work for a number of reasons I should not have needed to explain, but I had to explain why anyway, at least five times.

The day before our planned shoot day, I was on a wedding shoot and could not take any calls, which I had already explained to the client. But guess what? I got three phone calls from him during that day. At one point, I had to take a few minutes out to catch up on the phone calls and talk to the crew about what was going on. We all came to an agreement that shooting the next day clearly was not going to happen until everything was in place.

When I got home from the wedding, I called the client back and explained my reasoning for wanting to shoot on another day when we were more prepared. I tried reasoning with him and giving some input and new ideas. Like before, everything I said was just shot down.

I had had enough. I told the clients that they were welcome to take the footage I shot and give it to another editor. I even told them I would give back their deposit so they could find another videographer to finish it. Clearly I was not the person for it. What I thought was a civil way of clearing the air, turned into an argument during which I was called unprofessional and such. I calmly defended my team and myself and told the father to think about it. If he trusts me, then he should let me do my job the way I know how. He finally calmed down, but the worst still was not over. Yes, there's more.

We finally settled on a new date to wrap the video and got a good location. They compromised on a new plan. Everything was finally falling into place and I was actually relieved. The cinematographer with whom

I had been working could not make it, but I was able to find someone else to come and give me a hand. This person lives far away, but was willing to take the job because I was able to pay him. It was good for the both of us and we worked well together.

The day of the shoot came. I was getting ready to leave when I got a phone call from my replacement cinematographer telling me that his car broke down in the middle of the highway. I was convinced at that point that this project was cursed, but what could I do? The show had to go on. So, I found myself on my own, acting as director and cinematographer and pretty much everything else, in addition to dealing with this guy. Yeah, not exactly what I wanted to happen.

Of course, nothing I did was right. I kept feeling this guy's head looking over my shoulder at every moment. He was picking apart every little nook and cranny of the camera shot I had set up. Thank God, I was able to get a back-up crew member to at least come and help me. The rest of the shoot went according to plan and we wrapped. So, was the worst over yet? Think again. There was still post-production to deal with.

I spent the next couple of weeks working on the editing and it was going okay. It was a rough cut, so I knew it needed work. With clients like this though, I knew seeing something rough was not going to sit well with them. So I tried to make it look as complete as possible. I showed them the edit and to my surprise, they liked it! They had a lot of notes, but they liked it. What a relief!

I made the changes they asked for and sent them a second cut. The next day, I was on a shoot when I suddenly got a phone call from them, but I let it go to voicemail. Two minutes later, I got another phone call from a different number and also let it go to voicemail. Finally, yet another new number called me. Needless to say, I was fed up.

After my shoot, I checked my phone to find a three-and-a-half-minute message that was a complete rant about how unhappy the client was with the second cut. He felt the other edit was better and then asked to reshoot the singing scenes of the video. We talked about this for a while, a very long while. I told him that I would only reshoot if I got paid more, which he agreed to do.

We reshot those scenes, I got paid for the extra time and all seemed well. I did more editing on it. It was actually coming along nicely; they were very happy with it. Granted, it took quite a few edits until they were finally 100% satisfied. With every single edit, something new needed to be changed or they wanted to see what something looked like with different takes. I did twelve edits of the music video in the end, until they finally agreed it was complete. I guess I can't complain too much as the video has, thus far, been accepted into four festivals and even won an award. The award is what really made them happy.

You are probably wondering why in the hell I put up with such bullshit. Everybody with whom I have shared this story has told me that I have the patience of a saint. I cannot disagree with that; I just hate to give up or leave a client unhappy. As I look back, the situation was not totally the client's fault, but also my own. I should have been more aggressive in dealing with the client, more specific in my contract and even more prepared in shooting.

This is the lesson to be learned for those reading this: Know who you are going to be working with and what you are getting into before you do it. If something does not seem right to you, don't even bother wasting your time. When you do decide to accept a job, have a specific contract written out with all of the details about what the client wants. Most importantly, never undervalue your worth. You're going to be spending a lot of time and effort working for the client, so you want to make sure you get fair compensation for that time and effort. I also advise you to make sure you specify that the client is to receive no more than three previews or rough cuts. If you don't, you will be editing ten or twelve versions and your time will be wasted in a big way.

These are mistakes I have made and sometimes still do. Thankfully, since that project, I have implemented a more specific contract that has actually improved my relationships with clients. It also has helped me to create a final product with which both the client and I are happy.

If you want to find out more about working as a videographer, I would highly suggest checking out Brian Barnes' video seminar, *Succeeding in Corporate Videos*.[11] If you go to his website, you will find information about Brian, his work, and his course, for which you can get a thirty-percent discount if you use the following code (kindly provided by Brian): CHRSPR30. If you still don't believe me that videography is a great way to make money while building up your filmmaking career, Brian notes that one of the videographers who worked for him was Christopher Nolan. Yes, the director of *Memento*, *Inception*, *Interstellar* and *The Dark Knight*

---

[11] Succeeding in Corporate Videos:
www.brianbarnes.co.uk/py73hgrvs/index.html

trilogy was once a corporate videographer. Keep that in mind.

Chapter 7: The Importance of Feedback

"There are no two words in the English language more

harmful than 'good job'."

- Terence Fletcher, *Whiplash (2014)*

I could probably write a whole book about this subject. In any field you choose to pursue, you are going to be faced with feedback and criticism. This is especially true in creative fields like filmmaking. You have to grow a thick skin in this business, because feedback and criticism are part of the process of growth in your craft. I found that out the hard way when I was in college.

Until that point, I do not believe I had ever had anybody seriously look at my work in a critical way and give me feedback. I was just told that I did a good job. This is why I include that wonderful quote from *Whiplash*. It is such a powerful and true line. I often think being told that you did a good job is the equivalent of your parents hanging your drawing on the fridge when you were a kid, even though the drawing was not very good and they knew it.

I used this same analogy in *Still Life*.[12] There is a flashback scene showing the main character as a child taking Polaroid photos in his backyard. He excitedly shows his mother what he did and she hangs it up on the fridge. Meanwhile, in the present day, the main character is going through a period of questioning himself as an artist and whether or not he is good at photography. I based the film on my own questions about my abilities as a filmmaker.

When I made my first video projects for my college courses and it came time to present them to the class, the other students and professor would critique them. When it came time for my work to be critiqued, I always felt like I was standing naked in front of a large

---

[12] *Still Life*, directed by Chris Esper, 2012, available at www.storiesmotion.com

audience. I usually handled the professor's critique just fine, but when it came to my classmates, it was another story. I would feel a sense of being threatened or intimidated by them. Often my classmates would explain to me afterwards that their feedback was not meant to hurt, but to help. It really was not until making *Still Life* and experiencing the outside world in the business, that I got used to feedback and criticism, and even embraced them to a degree. Now, when I get a critique, I cannot say that I am thick-skinned, but I can certainly handle it in a professional manner. I can step back and see where the feedback makes sense and what could be fixed in my project.

I have always been a sensitive person and probably always will be, but the best way to handle situations like this is to avoid panic at all costs. Listen to the feedback you are getting and know that everyone has had to face criticism. Remember: you don't grow through praise. You grow through critique. That being said, there is a fine line between constructive criticism and destructive criticism.

For example, if you are editing a movie or writing a script, chances are you will want to get some feedback on your work. Be careful as to how many people you show your project to. Show it only to a select few, trustworthy peers whom you know are going to be honest with you and are looking to help you. If you show your work indiscriminately to multiple people, you end up hearing multiple opinions and never know to whom you should listen. You end up trying to listen to everybody. It becomes a situation where you are trying to please them and not yourself. Suddenly, your original vision is thrown away. Take every bit of criticism with a grain of salt, but don't deflect it completely either. In the end, it is your project and you need to be able to decide what is right for yourself and what is not.

This also brings up the point of surrounding yourself with good people. You have to surround yourself with people you can trust and whom you know are going to be honest, and not intentionally try to hurt you. Some will viciously criticize you and your work, possibly to make themselves feel better. That is why I advise you to choose those select few that are helpful and trustworthy. I will say more about this in the next chapter.

Chapter 8: Surround Yourself with the Right People

This is going to be a very short chapter because its message is simple. As a director, you can only be as good as your crew. You can have all the greatest skills in the world at directing actors and shooting scenes, but if your crew is not as skilled, competent and even trustworthy as you, this mismatch will show in the final product. Do not ever skimp on the people you work with. Don't always choose your friends. Before going into production, always make sure you have found the right person for each job.

It is very hard to find that one person who is skilled as a cinematographer and is also someone you can trust. Sometimes you might find a person who is very skilled but is not trustworthy or vice versa. When you are looking at any potential crew members, check their demo reels and resumes. Also, talk to others who have worked with these potential crew members in the past to find out what you can expect if you hire them. Then meet with these potential employees one-on-one to see how you click with them. If you aren't comfortable with any potential crew members in this situation, then working together on-set will not be any better.

Surround yourself with people who will make you look good and for whom you are willing to do the same in return. Remember, you should be collaborating with your crew, not challenging them or going against them. Before I went full-fledged into a directing career, I also did some crew work. I learned a lot about what qualities I would want or not want to have, not just in my crew, but also as a director.

Chapter 9: What it Means to be a Director

A couple of years ago, I came in contact with an actress/producer from L.A., who was originally from New England. At that point, she had just produced and acted in a feature that garnered a ton of attention and did very well on the festival circuit. I met her through a mutual friend who recommended me to direct a feature film she was going to be producing.

We talked for a little bit, but I was not too crazy about the script, so I passed on it. A few months later, she got another script, this time for a short film. She was interested in having me direct it. I actually liked the script. It wasn't perfect, but I felt it had a ton of potential and that I could bring a lot to it, so I agreed to the project. What I did not realize was that she wanted to start shooting within the next two weeks when she would be back in Boston.

The script was not very long, but for anything you make, you would hope for at least a month or more to prepare before going into it. We quickly gathered together a crew and arrived for the day of the shoot. I felt pretty good going into it, but things started to change very quickly. For some reason, the producer invited the writer to come onto the set. Normally, I would not mind this, as I usually enjoy working with the writer to collaborate on ideas and make sure their vision is on screen as much as my own. However, I was not aware that this would be happening. It kind of caught me off guard. I believe it was because of this added stress that I crumbled while making this film.

There were four main actors in the film and maybe twenty extras that showed up. Things started off fine, but slowly the producer and writer were against me. Every camera set-up and almost every idea I had was questioned by the two, who usually told me to do it a different way. Sure, I had discussed my ideas from the beginning, but they were a problem all of a sudden. I tried my best to respect them both, as this was the first time someone hired me to direct something that was not a project I started myself. Also, this was somebody from L.A. so I wanted to impress her.

At one point, I found myself arguing with them for five minutes over what kind of cup the main character would be drinking out of in this café we were shooting in. Yes, it was that ridiculous. I even saw the writer decorating the set with the set designer without asking for my input. When that happened, I just walked away and continued to shoot. It was utterly embarrassing having close to thirty people waiting for the director to tell them what the next shot was, while they were watching these arguments.

The rest of the day was slow-going because of situations like this. For example, the producer wanted to stick friends in as extras and have them deliver lines at points in the script that did not call for it. It made certain scenes lose the drama they carried. Finally, my production manager told them both to back off while I worked, adding that I was the director for a reason. It was a relief, but the damage was done.

After shooting ended, the producer found an editor. The editor put together a first rough cut. It was not too bad, at least in my opinion. It needed a lot of work, but there was potential there. I usually hate rough cuts because I just end up watching them with my hand over my face thinking, "Shit, is that what I did?" But I tried to be open-minded.

The producer felt that none of the footage had any redeeming qualities. She was especially upset about a shot where the main character looks directly at the camera. I did that intentionally because the script indicated that it was a point-of-view shot from across a table. Maybe I was totally wrong in how I interpreted it; we should have discussed that shot's setup in greater detail during pre-production. To be fair, this is why less than two weeks is not a sufficient amount of time for pre-production. Issues like this one could have been solved then and not on the day we shot.

The saddest part for me was that, from the producer's perspective, I was wrong on every point. It did not feel very fair, but what could I do? I had to take the blame.

This happened nearly three years ago. The film has still not seen the light of day because the producer wants to remake it with a different director. My name was taken off the IMDb listing of the film. To my knowledge, the film was never reshot. Two of the lead actors even tried to convince the producer to bring me back to finish it, but to no avail. This saddens me because the footage looked quite nice and the acting was very good, even given the short time we had to make it.

In retrospect, I could have done a much better job as a director. I don't believe I communicated well with the producer as to what I was hoping to achieve. At the same time, I felt bringing the writer into the mix was not helpful. That day was probably the worst I have ever felt on a set. I was not in control when I was supposed to be and was not confident in my vision.

When you are working as a director, you want to make sure you know what you want and how you want it. Take care of everyone around you, always be open to ideas, make sure everyone around you knows what you want, and most of all be confident. Being a director means being a fearless leader and not showing when you're scared or fearful. It's very easy to let your guard down under pressure. This could mean pretending that you're confident just to get through the day.

You have that one chance to get what you want. If you miss it and you're not happy, then nobody is going to look good on-screen. Be prepared to make mistakes and happy accidents. Come with a vision and all the success will follow. Also, be ready to be the open target for the positive and negative feedback you will receive. No matter how good or bad your film is, you will be the first person to take the hit.

One of my favorite movies about filmmaking is Francois Truffaut's *Day for Night*. There is a terrific scene where Truffaut, playing the director of the movie within the movie, is walking about his set to a narration expressing how he feels about directing the movie. Meanwhile, his crew members are bothering him left and right with question after question about what he is looking for. Truffaut's character says:

> *"Shooting a movie is a stagecoach ride in the Old West. At first, you hope for a nice trip. Soon you just hope you reach your destination! What is a film director? A man who's asked questions about everything. Sometimes he knows the answers."*[13]

It was this scene in the movie that made me love it as much as I do. I'm sure most of you reading this will also relate to that quote. Very often, you will have the

---

[13] *Day for Night*, directed by Francois Truffaut, full scene available here:
www.youtube.com/watch?v=1enCMgg7108

cinematographer asking you where you want the camera, actors asking about their motivation, the production designer asking you what color you want for the chairs, etc. It is like having multiple voices in your head. You're never sure who to answer first, or even if you're giving the right answers. It is like you are expected to know everything and have a solution to every problem. At least that is what I thought when I first started. But that cannot be further from the truth.

You don't have to know everything or be an expert. This is why you have crew members and actors. Without them, there is no movie. It's a collaborative effort. That doesn't sound too bad, right? Really it's not, as long as you don't make it too complicated or overthink it. Everyone on your team is on your side, which is why they come to you with questions. They want to please you and will come to the rescue when you don't have an answer for something.

Chapter 10: Technology and Filmmaking

In this day and age, it is not enough merely to have a website and business cards. I highly suggest also making skillful use of social media if you are going to get into the film business. Remember, you are a brand and an entity and you should sell yourself as such.

I'm constantly on Facebook, Twitter, Instagram, LinkedIn, and Google+. Using each one has gotten me some type of attention, and in some cases, jobs. Anytime you are working on something or planning a new project, make sure you post about it, as it will generate interest. I often feel like it's a second job to promote myself online because of how much effort goes into it.

By using social media, you are selling yourself and making yourself known. On the flipside, always read before you post and be extremely careful about what you say. For example, don't ever post about your political or religious beliefs on your Facebook page. I see a couple of filmmakers in my area always sharing their opinions about such subjects. Honestly, it is a huge turn-off. Be known for your talents, not your beliefs. If you want to share your feelings about a subject, you should save it for your work. Better yet, create a personal page where you can share these feelings with your friends. On my pages, I mostly post about film-related news because that's my business.

When it comes to promoting yourself, make sure you don't over-promote. I have seen many filmmakers who post non-stop about the same project over and over again and share their stuff in multiple groups without giving the readers a break. It becomes tiresome. Also, never announce anything new just to get likes, shares, etc. I once made the mistake of announcing a new project I was part of, but then the project went to a different director. Later I had someone ask me what was going on with it, which was kind of embarrassing. So, wait until you have your "T"s crossed and "I"s dotted before you post anything on your social media pages.

The most important thing about social media is to keep your posts short, sweet, to the point, and personal. When I say personal, I mean always show yourself in anything you promote. For example, if you are looking to raise money for a project on Indiegogo or Kickstarter, make sure you explain why the project is important to you. Do you have any idea how many filmmakers are out there these days? Tons. You have to be able to show why your project is worth investing in. Like I said earlier, anybody can make a movie now, but what separates you from the rest? Show that in anything you post. You have to break through the herd of filmmakers that stand in your way. This is why I feel that technology is both a blessing and a curse to the industry.

Technology is a blessing in that everyone today has easy access to make a movie and can readily get it out into the world. The curse, oddly enough, is exactly the same as the blessing. With so many people being able to make movies, you need to be able to stand out among everybody else. That's hard to do. The person who made that crappy film on YouTube could have connections in the industry and could get a big break, even if they don't demonstrate the level of skill or talent that you may have.

This is also partly why I have my 'vlog' and why I wrote this book. I want to share my story and my work with the world, while also helping others who wish to pursue a career in film. Just my 'vlog'[14] alone, I've received attention for a few of my projects from other filmmakers. Filmmakers have also contacted me to ask for feedback on their projects. You can do the same to gain a following.

With the Internet being a hub of free speech, everybody can make their opinions known rather quickly, so don't be surprised if your project gets some non-constructive negative comments. It has happened to me numerous times. I just ignore it or delete the comment. These people are known as "trolls" in the online community. Their mission is simply to get a rise

---

[14] *The Filmmaker's Journey* 'vlog'

out of you and get you to react. By responding, you are just making yourself look foolish. Remain professional and just ignore it. There is no sense in fighting back, because then they're getting what they want out of you, which is a reaction.

CHAPTER 11: DO IT FOR THE RIGHT REASONS

If there is one thing I cannot stand, it's when I hear directors talking about wanting to make millions of dollars, win multiple awards, get fame, etc. That is not what filmmaking is about. I believe that there are people who WANT to make movies and then there are people who HAVE to make movies. I have one filmmaking friend who is always going on and on about wanting to have his movies released by major studios, especially for his first feature film, and how he wants to be "filthy fucking rich."

Personally, I feel like I have to make movies. I just cannot imagine myself doing anything else in life. Without filmmaking, I often feel like I have nothing else to fall back on. Passion is what keeps me going and is what will keep you going, too. More importantly, it is the reason why you should be making movies. If you're doing it for a paycheck and fame, you are not doing it for the right reasons. For the first couple of years in your career, you will be making little to no income.

For the first three years or so in my career, I was doing a lot of volunteer work because I just wanted to get my foot in the door. I did whatever I could to get myself to the next level because I was passionate enough to do it. When I started getting paid, it was another incentive for me to continue working, but the money has always been secondary for me. This is especially true when I am directing something.

As a director, you want to make sure you don't just *like* the script. You have to LOVE the script. I cannot stress that enough. When you do a film that you're not crazy about, it is going to show up on-screen. I will be the first to admit that I have a couple of projects that I am not terribly proud of. The funny thing was that I knew I was not crazy about the scripts before getting into them.

So, why did I waste my time? Simply put, I wanted to pile up more directing work for my reel and my resume. I thought, "If I'm talented enough, maybe I can make it work. Maybe if I try new things in order to make them my own, I could turn them into something I love." I found out the hard way that if it's not love at first sight, then it is not worth pursuing. It is like being in a relationship with someone. You want to go for the person that you have feelings for and are falling in love with. You wouldn't go for the person that you don't have a connection to. So, why would you take just any script that comes your way?

There are so many times that I found myself working on a project and thinking to myself, "What the fuck am I doing? Why am I putting all this time and effort into something I don't care about?" Don't lower your standards to get more work. You're much better than that. Your time is valuable. If you are not pleased with a project you're working on, then don't do it. Go make that passion project you have always wanted to make.

Chapter 12: Final Thoughts

Filmmaking is one of the most difficult professions in the world. It is competitive, frustrating, stressful, and pretty much every other negative adjective you could think of. So why would any one want to get into it? Well, because it is also every positive adjective. It's fun, amazing, exhilarating, and so much more. The thing I love most about it is being a storyteller. I feel that I am more of an artist and storyteller than I am a technician or anything like that. I get such a rush from planning a project, to being on set, and then working with actors, and figuring out camera movements. I believe one has to be obsessed with the craft in order to turn it into a career. However, don't make filmmaking the only thing in your life.

The average person lives for over 27,000 days. Don't spend 20,000 of them doing nothing but film-related things. Go out, take a break and enjoy life. The reason I say that is because if all you know is movies, then there is not much for you to say in your stories. A great director, in my opinion, has had life experiences and can express them in a story without always relating everything back to movies. This is something I still deal with myself. Somehow, everything I do or talk about always relates back to work or just movies in general. There's nothing terribly wrong about that, but I think my stories would be more diverse and interesting if I got out more often and experienced more that life has to offer.

Have you heard the saying that too much of anything is no good? This applies to your career, too. If your friends invite you to go out to eat or go to a club and you have no major work to get done, then why not go out? You could experience something that gives you inspiration, either for the project you're working on, or for a new projects altogether.

Filmmaking is a journey. It is a long, hard road, but always worth it in the end when you're sitting in the cinema, seeing your film play to the members of an audience and listening to them react. It is one of the most satisfying feelings that one could ever have. It makes the rejection, failure, and hardship all the more worth it.

I hope my stories have given you a sense of both the highs and lows and realities of this career. Like me, your journey in filmmaking is far from over. I highly encourage you to start or continue your own journey. Get that camera in your hands and start shooting. And please send me your film when it's complete. I'd love to take a look! info.chrisesper@gmail.com.

This has been my story thus far, and it's only the beginning! This is an on-going journey that I am now prepared for. I love what I do and can't imagine myself doing anything else. I hope this piece has been helpful and enjoyable to read. I enjoyed writing it and sharing my thoughts and advice. Feel free to follow my work on my website[15] and my YouTube page under Stories in Motion[16].

Happy moviemaking!

---

[15] Chris Esper's website: www.storiesmotion.com

[16] Chris Esper's YouTube page

Appendix: References and Resources

Film Reviewers' Websites:

- *A Bucket of Corn -*
  http://www.abucketofcorn.com/

- *A Word of Dreams -*
  https://awordofdreams.wordpress.com/

- *Cinema Crazed -* http://cinema-crazed.com/blog/

- *Cinema Schminema -*
  http://cinemaschminema.com/

- *The Film Philosopher -*
  http://thefilmphilosopher.com/

- *The Final Cut -* https://www.youtube.com/user/Special Mark

- *Forest City Short Film Review –* forestcityshortfilmreview.blogspot.com

- *The Independent Critic -* http://theindependentcritic.com/home

- *IndyRed -* http://www.indyred.com/

- *Irish Film Critic -* http://irishfilmcritic.com/

- *Leah's Movie Lowdown –* http://www.leahsmovielowdown.com

- *The Local Film Network -* http://www.thelocalfilmnetwork.com/

- *Loud Green Bird -*
  http://loudgreenbird.com/

- *The Movie Waffler -*
  http://www.themoviewaffler.com/

- *Mr. Rumsey's Film Related Musings -*
  http://mrrumsey.com/

- *One Film Fan -* http://onefilmfan.com/

- *ProCreate -* http://teamprocreate.com/

- *(re)Search My Trash -*
  http://www.searchmytrash.com/

- *Reel Red Reviews -*
  http://reelredreviews.net/

- *Reviews by Amos Lassen -*
  http://reviewsbyamoslassen.com/

- *Rogue Cinema -* http://www.roguecinema.com/

- *Screen Critix -* http://screencritix.com/

- *Scott's Movies -* http://www.scottsmovies.com/

- *Snobby Robot -* http://snobbyrobot.com/

- *Sonic-Cinema -* http://www.sonic-cinema.com/news/

- *Strangers in a Cinema -* http://strangersinacinema.com/

- *UK Film Review -* http://www.ukfilmreview.co.uk/

- *Unsung Films -* http://www.unsungfilms.com/

- *VideoViews* -

  http://www.videoviews.org/

- *Watch This Space Film Magazine* -

  http://www.watchthisspacefilmmagazine.co.uk/

- *You've Got Film On You* -

  http://youvegotfilmonyou.weebly.com/

Websites to Submit to Film Festivals & Distribution:

- *Distribber* - www.distribber.com

- *Film Freeway* – www.filmfreeway.com

- *NoEntryFeeFestivals-*

  www.noentryfeefestivals.com

- *Short of the Week-*

  www.shortoftheweek.com

Esper/The Filmmaker's Journey   101

- *#TOFF: The Online Film Festival -* www.theonlinefilmfest.com

- *Withoutabox -* www.withoutabox.com

Websites for Filmmaking Advice & Tutorials:

- *D4Darious-* www.youtube.com/channel/UCYaIdC5pb kpECxXLjf0Lzaw

- *DSLRguide -* www.youtube.com/channel/UCzQ1L-wzA_1qmLf49ey9iTQ

- *Every Frame a Painting -* www.youtube.com/user/everyframeapai nting

- *FilmCourage-* www.youtube.com/user/filmcourage

- *Film Riot-* www.youtube.com/user/filmriot

- *Film Trooper -* www.filmtrooper.com

- *Filmmaker IQ -* www.filmmakeriq.com

- *FilmmakingProcess-* www.filmmakersprocess.com

- *Indie Film Hustle-* www.indiefilmhustle.com

- *No Film School -* www.nofilmschool.com

- *Phillip Bloom -* www.philipbloom.net

- *Brian Barnes* - www.brianbarnes.co.uk

Filmmaking Groups in the USA:

- *Austin Film Meet* (Austin, TX): http://www.austinfilmmeet.com/

- *Chicago Filmmakers* (Chicago, IL): http://chicagofilmmakers.org/

- *Film Independent* (Los Angeles, CA): http://www.filmindependent.org/

- *Florida Film Network* (Tampa Bay, FL): http://floridafilmnetwork.com/

- *Independent Filmmakers Coalition* (Kanas City, MO): http://www.ifckc.com/

- *Los Angeles Film & TV Meetup*: http://www.meetup.com/LAFilm-TV-Meetup-LAFTV/

- *Movie Making throughout the Bay!* (Concord,CA): http://moviemakingbay.com/

- *Rhode Island Film Collaborative* (Providence,RI): http://www.rifcfilms.com/

Classes & Career Opportunities:

- *John Truby* - www.truby.com

- *Kenneth Johnson*- www.kennethjohnson.us

- *Moving Picture Institute* - www.thempi.org

Books:

- *John Badham on Directing* by John Badham, Michael Weise Productions, 2013.

- *Painting with Light* by John Alton, University of California Press, 1995.

- *Save the Cat! The Last Screenwriting Book You'll Ever Need!* by Blake Synder, Michael Wiese Productions, 2005.

- *Short Films 2.0: Getting Noticed in the YouTube Age* by Mikel J. Wisler, DoxaNoûs Media, 2016.

- *Story: Style, Structure, Substance, and Principles of Screenwriting* by Robert McKee, ReganBooks, 1997.

- *The War of Art: Break Through the Blocks and Win Your Creative Battles* by Steven Pressfield, Black Irish Entertainment LLC, 2002.

- *The Writer's Journey: Mythic Structure for Writers, 3rd Edition* by Christopher Vogler, Michael Wiese Productions, 2007.

CPSIA information can be obtained at www.ICGtesting.com
Printed in the USA
BVOW06s1922220916

463020BV00019B/302/P